MW00425400

I Tried
(And Other Poems, Too)

All the best,
Steven Kent

I Tried
(And Other Poems, Too)

by

Steven Kent

Cover design by Shay Culligan
Cover photo by Steven Kent

ISBN: 978-1-63980-372-9

Kelsay Books
502 South 1040 East, A-119
American Fork, Utah 84003
Kelsaybooks.com

Thanks to Dr. David George and Dr. Barry Milligan,
two outstanding professors who taught me take poetry seriously
even when, as in this collection, its primary purpose is to amuse.

Thanks to Melissa Balmain and Jerome Betts,
editors at *Light Poetry Magazine* and *Lighten Up Online,*
respectively, for publishing many of my submissions
and for providing great feedback and insights.
"The Editors Who Love My Work" is for them.

Thanks most of all to my wife Jeni
and our adult children Grant, Davis, Bennett, and Mina
for their love and support.
"Can't Get Better" and "All the Noise" is dedicated to them.

Acknowledgments

Thank you to the following publications, where versions of these poems previously appeared:

Light Poetry Magazine: "I Tried," "Late to the Party," "Losing My Religion(s)," "Mr. In-Between" (Some headline poems were featured as *Light* Poems of the Week)

Lighten Up Online: "A Foodie Lament," "Baby, It's Cold Inside," "The Cake Aisle of Applebee's," "Memoirese," "The Next Small Thing," "The Plague," "Right on Time," "To Kill With Kindness," "Unacknowledged"

Philosophy Now: "At My Leisure"

Contents

Act IV: Headline Poems

Act V: Random Discursions

Act I: Human, All Too Human

In which the author contemplates personal relationships,
both romantic and filial

Can't Get Better

There has to be a garment which
Can't be improved, not by a stitch;
A song some great composer wrote
Where one would never change a note.

The work of Shakespeare as it stands
Won't be enhanced by other hands,
And no new artist can beguile
Like Leo's *Mona Lisa* smile.

The Parthenon, a Frank Lloyd Wright—
Both bathe in sheer perfection's light.
In sum, to wit, my point, the gist:
My love, you should be on this list!

All the Noise

We can stay up as late as we're able;
We can make all the noise that we choose,
Watch whatever we want to on cable,
Eat and drink lots of junk food and booze.

No example to set! We can slack now,
Live the way we remember, my dear.
Every freedom we had once is back now,
And I sure wish the kids were still here.

A Tale of Two Artists

Your genius, darling, I revere;
I know you feel the same for mine.
But someday push may come to shove
And we can't both get all the love.
If one of us alone may shine,
It really must be me, I fear.

Right On Time

Alarm goes off, I rise and leave my cozy sleeping spot;
It's been this way for years and years, 6:30 on the dot.
I fetch my robe from off the hook, then wash and shave my face
Before I comb my hair until there's not one out of place.

I drink my coffee black and hot, 6:45 precisely,
And if it takes five minutes more, that won't do near as nicely.
The eggs must be well-scrambled, dry, the bacon should be lean.
(My love, you say *Go with the flow.* Whatever do you mean?)

Ten-minute shower, then I dress and leave at half-past 8:00,
Arriving at the office never early, never late.
I lunch at 12:00 exactly, back to work as clock strikes 1:00
Until the stroke of 5:00 p.m., and then my day is done.

5:45, I'm back at home, where Cindy's at the sink,
And right on time she takes my coat and offers me a drink
Before she serves up dinner, 6:00 o'clock—that's our routine.
(My love, you say *God, loosen up!* Whatever do you mean?)

The kids head to their room at 9:00; I tuck them in each night.
We talk for fifteen minutes, then I turn out each one's light.
Downstairs I stay for one more hour, then right to bed I go
And straight to sleep; what happens past 11:00, I don't know.

Some say a person has no need to regiment his life
The way I've done, but really I just do it for my wife—
She so adores the way each day is run like a machine.
(My love, you say *I'm leaving you!* Whatever do you mean?)

They Grow Up So Slow

Is there a fount of boundless joy
Quite like a surly teenage boy?
His one true equal as a churl
Could only be a teenage girl.

On Second Thought

I don't want to know where you're going;
  I don't long to know where you've been.
I've no more concern for your welfare,
  Don't care if you lose or you win.

Romance that we knew is long buried;
  It died and you killed it, not me.
I'm all out of ways to reject you;
  How clear can I possibly be?

But wait, now you're telling me something
  You think I just might want to know
About the estate of your uncle—
  I'll give you five minutes or so.

He left you some ten million dollars
  And a platinum mine overseas?
He altered his will and he named you
  His heir? Tell me more, if you please.

Turns out that he also had villas
  In Greece and the southwest of Spain?
A vineyard in Napa, another
  In France with the finest champagne?

He kept several vintage Ferraris
  At his house in the Hamptons, you say?
And the lawyer just called to inform you
  The estate will be yours any day?

You know, dear, we've been much too hasty
  In throwing away good romance.
Oh love, take my hand, I'm all yours now—
  We *really* must give this a chance!

Easy to Remember

I quote Plato's *Republic* and Ari's First Cause,
    The *Decameron, Hamlet,* and more,
Know the table of elements, Newton's three laws,
    Ancient exploits of Caesars galore,
Every president, pontiff, and potentate yet,
    Plus the order they served in, and when.
Ah, but some things I strangely still seem to forget—
    Darling, tell me your birthday again?

A Family Affair

Young Stuart Morgan passed away,
And some were later heard to say
The funeral was the talk of Sawyer Station.
His wife and boys by casket stood
With friends from their old neighborhood,
When came a most upsetting revelation.

A woman with two girls walked in;
She said, "My name is Tammy Lynn,"
And that's when everything got really twisted.
For Stuart had a secret, see:
To wit, a second family,
And neither knew the other one existed.

Such drama! Oh, the drama there,
With screaming, scratching, pulling hair;
Three cops were called to separate the mothers.
The kids looked on in horror till
One turned and said, "That's Beth; I'm Jill—
Apparently we're sisters now and brothers."

But once the shock wore off, both wives
Got new perspective on their lives,
And each agreed the other was deserving
Of better than she got from Stu.
Moreover, they decided to
Try something certain locals found unnerving:

Though left with little by that louse,
They pooled their funds and bought a house
Where all his kids could live and grow together.
In laughter, tears, and daily chores,
This pair of Stuart's paramours
Discovered they were birds of common feather.

The lesson here: A heartache mends.
They all became the best of friends,
These children and their weirdly widowed mamas.
Sans Stu, life's better every day—
I hear last year they saw L.A.
And now they've booked a cruise to the Bahamas.

Words Fail Me

My love, I praise your pulchritude,
But do you thank me? You do not.
Instead you simply say *how rude*
(Which lately you say quite a lot).
So then I try to speak about
That perspicacity of yours,
But right away you start to pout
And storm out, slamming all the doors.
Your verisimilitude, pet,
Deserves great honor every day—
Please tell me why you're so upset
With all these compliments I pay.

I call you sedulous and more:
   Insouciant, veracious,
Punctilious down to the core,
   A mulier most gracious,
And yet you swear you never hear
   The pillow talk you long for.
I've come to fear—it's true, my dear—
   You all my words are wrong for.

Cold Shoulder

"From now on I'll be vegan," I told her—
She would otherwise not let me hold her.
When she's gone, though, I cheat:
Not on her, but with meat!
(Were I bolder, I'd get the cold shoulder.)

Baby, It's Cold Inside

My pet, take off your sweaters—I
Feel amorous this very hour.
These passions rise; I know the power
Is off (the price of heat is high),

But let us choose to celebrate
Today within our downy bed,
With chilly pillows for the head
And blankets for our frigid state.

What's that? You simply won't undress
As long as you can see your breath?
My dear, I fear we'll freeze to death
If you refuse to acquiesce.

Come live with me and be my love
And we will all the pleasures prove,
Though not until you first remove
At least two layers and a glove.

Act II: The Aging Process

In which the author confronts the inevitable
and frankly does not like what he sees

Reunion

It's been full forty years, and so
To class reunion now I go.
My hair is cut, my suit is pressed
(I like to be my very best).
I don't suppose I've stayed as trim
As those who hang around the gym;
I'm sure I will not look as good
As jocks from my old neighborhood,
But we all do what we can do,
And what the heck, I'll make it through—
Appearance, I have learned at length,
Has never been my major strength.

Will I see Carol? Karen? Jill?
I often think about them still,
And Christie with her flaxen hair,
Tight sweaters cut way down to there,
Francine (who wore my old class ring),
Beth Ann (she taught me everything),
Sweet Connie (no, not *that* one, fool)—
So many girls I loved in school.
All these, and some who came before,
I hope I'll find behind this door.

But wait; man, something isn't right,
Or maybe we don't have good light.
I see a hundred heads of grey—
I'm shocked; I don't know what to say.
Is this the room, the time, the place?
I fail to recognize one face!

These couples, who I swear could be
My uncle's age, all stare at me
As if they've never seen a guy
So young and virile. Tell me why
I'm now surrounded everywhere
By wrinkles, baggy skin, and hair
Grown thin (or worse, that waved *adieu*).
Can this be real? Can this be true?
I feel the very blood turn cold—
Good God, my peers have gotten *old!*

Lesson Learned

When I was young and knew it all, I'd find myself astonished
At wisdom I could offer to the others I admonished
On each and every topic: true religion, child-rearing,
Love, politics, and finance (I could be quite domineering).

How very, very long ago! Today's another story.
No longer do I revel in this rush of youthful glory,
For time reveals the limits of our meager comprehension;
Revising old opinions now demands my full attention.

Go West, Old Man

Who recalls the Brooklyn Dodgers?
Just a few disgruntled codgers
Sore as ever, now as then
(You really can't go home again),
While Sandy Koufax lives today
And walks the beach in West L.A.

Late to the Party

I've always been late to the party,
  Whatever the party might be.
New styles come and go, then a memo
  That somehow I never do see.
I did not stop dancing to disco,
  My haircut is forty years old,
And double-knit "vintage" apparel
  Still keeps me quite warm from the cold.

The ties in my closet are bolder
  And wider than any you'll find;
They match the lapels on my jackets,
  All poly blends, all the same kind.
My worn patent leather brown slip-ons
  Beat all the top brands at the store—
You *cannot* find shoes and belt matching
  At quality shops anymore.

It's tough now replacing shag carpet
  Or fixing my big waterbed;
Corinthian leather is fading
  Just like the tight perm on my head.
In movies I watch only classics;
  TV? I'll take more of the same.
I simply don't care for the new stuff;
  Past '80 it's all pretty lame.

T. Bennett still plays on the hi-fi,
  J. Mathis, J. Jones, and all such,
G. Lightfoot, E. John, and J. Denver
  (The Captain and T. not so much).
My books? Pynchon, Pirsig, and Mailer
  Plus *Roots*—that's a given, I'd say—
And *Jonathan Livingston Seagull*
  (I swear I'll read *that* one someday).

33

I'll always be late to the party
   No matter the when or the where,
And though I'm long due for an update,
   To tell you the truth I don't care.
So yes, I'm behind in my fashion—
   I don't go for cutting-edge verve—
But given how trends all recycle,
   I'll soon be ahead of the curve!

Health Walk

I walk to pub, not all that far;
One pint, then on my way.
I know that I could take the car
But it's a sunny day.

Which clearly makes this *exercise*
(Or so it seems to me),
And thus I think I might be wise
To stay for two or three.

Now if a stroll to sip one brew
Can bring good health to men,
Imagine all that *four* could do:
A champion's regimen!

One has to find such helpful tricks
To keep in fighting trim.
My uncle swears by five or six—
I'll take a page from him.

I aim to die a ripe old gent,
Perhaps at 103.
If I can keep this athlete's bent
Just think how fit I'll be!

Much More Nothing

Some tell me they're bored in retirement:
  One day's like another, they state,
With nothing by way of appointments
  And nothing of note on their plate.

No calendar entries, commitments,
  Or labors to check off their chart.
More nothing from morning till evening
  And nothing to finish or start.

But I have a different perspective,
  Which nothing can alter, it's true:
Each day I can't wait for tomorrow—
  I've so much more nothing to do!

Zero Birthday

A zero birthday come again?
This means I'm even older, then.
The last time round (I still recall)
I hadn't lost much hair at all;
The step was firm, the eyes were keen,
But something happened in between.
My mind was sharp, I knew no fears—
Alas, it's been a tough ten years.

Act III: Philosophy and Other Diversions

In which the author struggles vainly
to grasp the elusive Big Picture

Unacknowledged

Poets are the unacknowledged legislators of the world.
—Percy Bysshe Shelley

The poets have been losing in the legislative game;
We're unacknowledged still, now more than ever.
But surely Shelley knew our fate would likely stay the same;
Was he sincere or simply being clever?

Imagine if his observation went the other way!
How perfect this might be—the world will know it
If ever we should live to see that bright and shining day
The statesman is an unacknowledged poet.

Canon Fodder

I don't believe I'd like to be a saint;
Some things I am, some things I really ain't.
It's way too much responsibility,
Too many years of dreadful company.

I'm sure ascetic life is very fine,
But never would I want it to be *mine.*
The martyr's crown is too big for my head;
I'll settle for a jester's cap instead.

Still, I have no intention to deny
Great glory if it's offered by and by:
I know my name will not a parish grace,
Yet I say prayers each morning just in case.

Ya Gotta Know the Territory

My cousin's in a klezmer band (it has a Yiddish name).
They're very good; he couldn't wait to join.
But they can't get arrested—not one gig, and that's a shame;
Seems no one dances *freylekhs* in Des Moines.

Don't Tread On Me won't fly in San Francisco or L.A.
No rainbow flags in Lima or Moline.
No foreign films in Fargo, while at Harvard (so they say)
Truck rifle racks are few and far between.

Ya gotta know the territory—that's the way it goes;
Don't swim away your life against the tide.
The grass is always greener 'cross the fence, you might suppose
Whenever it's not growing on your side.

Mr. In-Between

I'm Mr. In-Between, said he,
And my position's very clear:
I'll straddle any line in sight,
My feet on both the Left and Right.
I'll be the man you'd have me be,
And say the words you want to hear.

I'll lower taxes just for you
And raise them on some other Joe.
Since you work hard while he does not,
You'll get much more of what he's got,
But then the same I'll have to do
For him in fairness, don't you know.

God bless our troops—I raise my voice!
Still, I can't bring myself to vote
To raise their pay or ease their load,
For in the middle of the road
I'm firm—I dare not make a choice,
Or stand up now and rock the boat.

The rights of all minorities
I do support—in fact, with pride—
Though I won't ever plead their cause
Or try to alter unjust laws,
For doing so might well displease
Some voters on the other side.

I have my principles, dear friend,
And these in stone are firmly set
Unless you tell me you object,
And then I'll simply resurrect
The ones I lived by last weekend
Or find some new ones, better yet.

I'm Mr. In-Between, said he,
And my position's plain as day:
I'm here, I'm there, I'm back and forth,
I now declare for what it's worth
That I will always, *always* be
The same tomorrow. Let us pray.

Losing My Religion(s)

I make a bad Buddhist, I know.
I aim to be better and still
Despite all my trying
Mosquitos come flying,
And I go right in for the kill.

I make a bad Hindu, I know.
I'm all for nirvana and bliss,
But I'll be frustrated
If reincarnated
To live again lower than this.

I make a bad Muslim, I know.
I *so* love both bacon and beer,
And travel to Mecca
Would leave me a wreck, a
Most pitiful pilgrim, I fear.

I make a bad Christian, I know.
I'm lacking in mercy and grace,
And like the disciples
I'm hung up on trifles
And miss what's in front of my face.

I make a bad pagan, I know.
Though Earth I do long to protect,
It's unrealistic
To be pantheistic
And therefore I don't genuflect.

I make a bad Buddhist, I know.
I've been awfully patient somehow
But frankly, Gautama,
I'm done with the drama—
I want my Enlightenment *now!*

The Lilies

The lilies neither toil nor spin,
Yet Solomon would not have been
Arrayed like these, or so we're told:
They live in peace, both young and old,
While humans hustle to and fro
And push and pull and stop and go.

Beware the energetic man,
A slave to his own master plan
To win the race against a rat—
No earthly good can come of that.
Let vain ambition learn to yield
Before these lilies of the field.

At My Leisure

Leisure is the mother of Philosophy, some say;
If it's true my future's looking great. Oh
Man, with all this free time on my hands most every day,
Surely I'll become another Plato.

Doing nothing all day long is quite a lot of work!
Praying now my genie in her bottle
Comes out quick and with a fairly firm-but-gentle jerk
Turns me to a modern Aristotle.

Fully rested, heavy thoughts all worked out in my head,
Then my metaphysics might endure. Us
Humans need a teacher—when at last I leave my bed,
I'll be right up there with Epicurus.

Note: My Muse won't visit if I cannot hear her voice,
So I beg you please to be discreet. She
Takes an all-or-nothing stance and leaves me little choice,
Yet I yield, that I may be like Nietzsche.

Leisure is the mother of Philosophy, you bet;
Humbly will I play my modest part. The
Peace and quiet I require might seem a lot, and yet
I need these if I'm to rival Sartre.

The Plague

Well, Camus wrote *The Plague* (or *La Peste*)
Then he said as he puffed out his chest,
"Jean-Paul Sartre, *mon frere,*
Wrote *Nausee.* To compare:
A good book, but *mon Dieu,* mine is best!"

This Split's Bananas

Mind and body torn asunder,
R. Descartes' historic blunder.
Ancient Greeks would pitch a fit
To learn of his Cartesian Split:
Cogito, ergo sum? Guess maybe
You forgot the body, Baby!

The Readiness Is All

I shall be born when and where I want,
and I do not choose to be born in Lowell
                    —James Whistler

If ever we should come to understand
How we might choose our time and place of birth,
Immortal soul
In full control,
We're bound to ride that train for all it's worth.

How sweet to say *This is not as I planned,*
To move the fateful hour and the address,
For then we find
Real peace of mind
That comes with one short lifetime to express.

And if the power lies within our hand
To join the world our way right from the start,
It seems to me
We ought to be
Allowed as well to choose how we depart.

I Tried

I tried to be a guru but the hours were too long
With meditation, prayers, and mindful thinking.
The money and the groupie girls were great, don't get me wrong,
But then they said I'd have to give up drinking.

I tried to be an idler, but the labor was too much;
Each day the odds of my success diminished.
With this and that and how and why and when and where and such,
I never really knew when I was finished.

I tried to be a sculptor, next a painter, then a bard,
My lack of any talent notwithstanding.
It wasn't that the work, per se, was really all that hard,
But self-promotion proved much too demanding.

I tried to be a dreamer but the dream just wouldn't call;
I never gained that land of milk and honey.
Imagine no possessions, it's not hard to do at all
Said someone with a pocketful of money.

I tried to be a critic, with an arbitrary pen
Dispensing deadly darts of fiery censure.
But being judge and jury left me jaded in the end
And robbed me of the taste for that adventure.

I tried to be myself at last; so far it's going well.
I play the role with pride yet self-effacement.
I hope the show goes on for years, though you can never tell—
Tomorrow they might send in my replacement.

Act IV: Headline Poems

In which the author peruses the news of the day
and responds in verse to our absurd world

The Great Masters 2.0

We don't need another Michelangelo: In Italy, it's robots' turn to sculpt
(July 2021)

Take note, young sculptors, Venice to Milan:
Your genius and your skill are no more needed,
For these machines work harder than you can
And won't complain when they get superseded.

They may not have a vision, style, or grace,
Or any other trait that art requires,
But we can fit a dozen in one space
And run them round the clock—how *that* inspires!

And who's to say a hundred years from now
(For those of us who might be down-the-roaders)
That we'll recall what "art" was anyhow—
By that point all the artists will be coders.

Strength in Numbers

New Zealand police break up one-person anti-lockdown protest
(August 2021)

What do we want? No answer came.
When do we want it? More of same.
There's strength in numbers! Good one, kid.
They can't arrest us all! They did.

Get Me to the Church
(To the tune of "Get Me to the Church on Time")

Indian couple float to wedding in cooking pot after floods in Kerala
(October 2021)

I'm gettin' married in the morning
Just like a young man in my prime.
Rivers are rising;
We're enterprising—
Get me to the church on thyme.

Rains have been falling here for hours,
Water's too high for us to climb.
Flood of emotion;
I have a notion—
Get me to the church on thyme.

If we are tardy they'll understand,
But we are hardy—boys, lend a hand!

Nothing can keep us from that altar;
Soon all the bells are gonna chime.
Hall's fully booked now,
My goose is cooked now—
Get me to the church on thyme.

Our friends are doting—give them a show.
Now we are floating—come on, let's go!

Looks like it's gonna be our season,
Looks like today will be sublime.
Babe, we can book there,
We'll take the cookware—
Get me to the church, get me to the church,
Please, please get me to the church on thyme.

Pop Heart

Secret Piety: New Show Reveals Andy Warhol's Catholic Roots
(October 2021)

The parties, fame, the glitz, the dope;
Communion, saints, the Church, the Pope—
The world is too much with me, yet
I never shall my faith forget.
Can I commit my soul to art
As well as to the Sacred Heart?
One cannot God and Mammon serve,
But then again, who has my nerve?

OK Computer

Is it okay? The bot that gives you an instant moral judgment
(November 2021)

The words of great philosophers, though prone to human folly,
  Are moral more than merely epigram,
But only if they lived and walked among us here, by golly—
  Said no sage yet, "I think, therefore I RAM."

Seeing Stars

Experience: A meteorite crashed on to my bed
(February 2022)

I've seen some shooting stars in bed—
   Come on, you know the feeling!
But this one went straight to my head
   (Or tried to) through the ceiling.

In the Bag (or, The In Bag)

KFC's £198 Twister Holder touted as next it bag
(April 2022)

Chanel, Hermes, Vuitton, and Prada—
Handbags I'll have none of, *nada.*
So long Coach, goodbye to Fendi;
Now a brand-new name is trendy.
Who's the hottest? Fashion branders,
Listen up: It's Colonel Sanders.

I Shine When I'm Dull

Experience: I am the dullest man in Britain
(June 2022)

Choose a bore, who's a bore?
One Kevin Beresford
Photographs roundabouts,
Car parks, and such.

Ambling through life rather
Uncharismatically,
Winning awards for his
Dullness—too much!

Come Fly
(To the tune of "Come Fly With Me")

The super-rich who have absolute disregard for the planet
(July 2022)

Come fly with me, come fly, let's fly away.
I'm rich! My rule: burn exotic fuel,
Let the common people pay.
Come fly with me, come fly, come fly away.

Come fly with me, we'll float to Hollywood.
In La-La Land there's an indie band,
And I hear they're pretty good.
I'll never fly commercial like I should.

Once I get you up there where the hoi polloi can't go
It's my show,
Don't you know.
Once I get you up there I'll be taking you cross-town;
We'll come down
When my Instagram is updated.

Weather-wise, who cares what this might do.
The carbon burn isn't my concern—
Baby, screw the CO_2!
It's perfect for a pointless afternoon, I say;
Come fly with me, come fly, let's fly away.

What Should We Wear to Picket?

*Strippers are standing up: Los Angeles dancers move to unionize
with actors group*
(August 2022)

Let's take a pole, girls: Unionize,
   Or just keep dancing 'round these fights?
Well, Stormy? Sapphire? Nays or ayes?
   Don't let them strip us of our rights!

A Fin Mess

Epaulette sharks able to walk on land evolving to better survive
climate crisis
(August 2022)

I saw *Jaws* at the mall as a kid.
It was scary; I ran home and hid.
So I don't care to see
A shark walk, no sirree—
Captain Quint, do that thing you once did!

The Wild Crew Yonder

Two Air France pilots suspended after midair fight prompts cabin crew
to intervene
(August 2022)

Please fasten seatbelts now, as we
Expect a bumpy flight and such.
Outside it's nice as it can be;
Inside the cockpit, not so much.

Air France would like to make it clear
You're very safe; I'll say this twice.
We do not need a doctor here,
Although a bouncer might be nice.

It's Not About the Money

Money isn't important! Take it from Google's multimillionaire CEO
(September 2022)

Now listen, plebes—I'm sorry, *valued workers*—
We're all in this together, understand?
At first we said we wanted idle shirkers
To chill at work; that didn't go as planned.

So here's the deal: You'll learn to live on less here
(Though still you must be at our beck and call).
I make six mil, but—can I just confess here?—
It's not about the money, not at *all*.

Pub Work/Pub Life Balance

What's it like working from the pub?
(October 2022)

Hey boss, you hear me now? Okay,
Let's talk about this merger deal.
Due diligence I've done; I feel—
Kate, give me fish and chips today.

Where were we? Right, the merger mess.
I really think we should proceed;
We've got the funding, now we need—
Kate, how about a Guinness, yes?

So here's the thing, Boss, I won't lie:
The competition's closing in,
And if we ever hope to win—
Kate, I could go for shepherd's pie.

Hold on, you're telling me right here
I'm off the project? Reason is
I'm too distracted for this biz?
Hey, Kate, I'm gonna need more beer!

A Head of Her Time

Iceberg lettuce in blond wig outlasts Liz Truss
(October 2022)

The lettuce lives, while Liz as PM's dead—
Won by a nose, but soon lost by a head.

The Naughty List

Whisper list contains 40 politicians never to accept a drink from, MP claims (November 2022)

Girl, find a public place, a park or station,
If you and he must talk of legislation.
Don't meet him in his office or a bar
Or any place no other people are.
He wields a lot of power, so much leverage;
Decline if he should offer you a beverage,
For God knows what'll happen if you drink—
Back-bench he's called, but not for what you think!

License to Thrill

Diet of rainbows and sunlight: California girl given first-ever unicorn license
(December 2022)

Miss Madeline, we do insist
Before we put you on our list
That, if one ever should be born,
You'll love and raise this unicorn.

You'll take it yearly to the vet,
This purely theoretic pet
That lives alone in children's thoughts,
And make sure it gets all its shots.

You'll teach it what it needs to know,
You'll feed it what it needs to grow,
And—please forgive our breach of taste—
You'll clean up all its rainbow waste.

I Guess That's Why They Call It Sing Sing

Prisoner fighting extradition 'bullied' by cellmates singing
'Leaving on a Jet Plane'
(January 2023)

Big meanies! They refuse to stop
Tormenting me with vintage pop.
"Jet Plane" might leave a mental scar,
But "Jailhouse Rock"? A bridge too far!
That con man's got a decent voice,
Though I can't get behind his choice.
The song he sang is somewhat strange:
"I Fought the Law" ain't in his range,
And OMG, I dread the day
These guys bust out "I'll Fly Away!"

A Minor Inconvenience

The US Labor Department found children as young as 13 years old
working in sanitation jobs at meatpacking plants
(February 2023)

Repeal the laws and drop the fines
And get these youngsters to the mines!
It's time we turn back history's page
To let them earn an honest wage,
For work will teach both sage and fool
So much he'll never learn in school.

Our groceries, diner kitchens, pet shops,
Mills and farms and factory sweatshops
Need cheap labor, yes indeedy.
Unions? Kids, now *don't get greedy!*

The Best Laid Plans

NASA tracking asteroid that could ruin Valentine's Day in 2046
(March 2023)

From science, now some gloomy expectations:
In years to come I'm fated for frustrations.
All dashed, my hopes of intimate relations;
I guess I'll call and cancel reservations.

Working Title

King Charles gives Prince Edward 'Duke of Edinburgh' title
(March 2023)

Prince Ed will never sit upon my throne,
So he deserves a dukedom of his own.
The job description's really not exact—
No work's required of any kind, in fact.

Justice Is Served

*Virginia prisoners who used toothbrush to escape
caught at pancake restaurant*
(March 2023)

One wonders: Was the plan itself so awful?
Or did they simply lose their nerve and waffle?
In any case, let's keep in mind what mattered:
Both crooks have been a-salted, whipped, and battered.

Love Will Find a Wei

Chinese startup invents long-distance kissing machine
(March 2023)

Will love live on with you and me
   Apart? My darling, mine'll.
Oh, sweet as wine your kiss would be
   If wine were made from vinyl.

Act V: Random Discursions

In which the author discovers how many of his poems
refuse to fit into the other four categories

The Poet of Comic Persuasion

The poet of comic persuasion
  Will sense condescension at times
From oh-so-so serious writers
  Unversed in both humor and rhymes.

Iambic pentameter's dated,
  They sniff. *Anapestics? Passé!*
And limericks? Thank God The New Yorker
  Disdains juvenilia today!

Alas, they forget Dorothy Parker
  And frankly the great Ogden Nash,
Who said more in two metered couplets
  Than those who, when closing, go off on a tangent,
    extending the line and then filling whole pages
    with angst-laden free balderdash.

Shorties

At The Pizzeria

Cheese?
Please.

The Hangman's Offer Rejected

Rope?
Nope.

Undergraduate Weekend

Math,
Plath,
Bath.

Panic! At The Campsite

Bear!
Where?
There!

A Foodie Lament

Unsalted nuts and decaf coffee,
Low-cal beer, no-sugar toffee,
Bread from sprouts and plant-based meats,
Non-dairy cheese and all such "treats"
Keep far away—though people buy 'em,
I have no desire to try 'em.

Walden claims that life's about
Those things we learn to live without,
But let him not be misconstrued:
Thoreau did not speak here of food,
And while such fare some folk might savor,
I prefer the kind with flavor.

Fore Hearth and Home

I wanted a house on a golf course
  But found all the prices too high,
And then I discovered a suburb
  For frugalish folk such as I.
A new kind of sport-centered living
  Where athletes like me can unwind.
The houses are small, with good reason:
  Golf here is the miniature kind.

My dining room faces a windmill,
  The figure-eight's easy to see,
And clown mouth is close to those bushes—
  Like all the holes here, it's par three.
I pop some nice bread in the toaster
  And brew up a coffee for one;
I'll play a few rounds and be finished,
  Back home before breakfast is done.

We don't have a cart or a caddy;
  One putter is all that we use,
While orange balls and scorecards and pencils
  Are more in demand here than shoes.
If duffers put balls in the water
  Despite having carefully tried,
It's not all that tough to retrieve them—
  The hazard's a mere three feet wide.
When tragedy strikes on the fairway
  (There's always the Law of Old Murph)
We never call in an attendant,
  Just glue down some new Astroturf.

We meet at the clubhouse each evening
  (By "clubhouse" I mean the beer tent),
Then lift a small glass to each other
  And wonder where all the time went.

So if you like lifestyle and leisure
  But don't want them too overblown,
Come putt down some roots here at Fun World,
  The best little golf club in town!

I've Got a Crèche or Two
(To the tune of "I've Got a Crush on You")

Of all the decorations
For Yuletide celebrations
We own, one kind alone
Did not go to the attic,
And now I'm getting static
From she who married me:
I need every table clear by springtime, love,
With all Christmas bric-a-brac put up above.
My darling wife is fairer;
I might have made an error.
Now she won't let it be. . . .

I've got a crèche or two, my oh my,
On the shelves and mantel way up high.
I never had apprehension
That my decor could cause so much tension.
Should I store, should I stow
Jesus, Mary, Joseph? I guess so.
My love just wants to look fresh,
But I have got a crèche, oh baby, or two.

Remember My Name

I'm Eleanor of Aquitaine,
But you can call me Betty Blaine.
I haven't gone by Eleanor
Since I left France in 1204.

I'll tell you now: In my next life
I won't be someone else's wife.
Though kings might woo me, I'll refuse
And take whatever name I choose.

Loathe Not the Limerick

You long to create lots of laughter?
Of mirth you'd be much more a crafter?
Forget all the gimmericks,
Go forth and write limericks
(But do keep your day job hereafter).

Memoirese

The young memoirist has her say,
  But isn't it ironic—
She's twenty-two if she's a day,
  A far cry from iconic.

She stars in some new TV show
  Now going on two seasons,
And in this time she's "learned to grow"
  For oh so many reasons.

Such wisdom here! Knows even more
  Than back when she was twenty.
(Just wait until she's twenty-four;
  She'll be a cognoscente.)

An author once would earn that name
  By force of reputation,
But now the slightest claim to fame
  Is cause for publication.

So friend, remember when you write:
  Celebrity is power.
Though it can come as fast as night
  And leave within the hour.

Pedestrian

You're a manifest equestrian;
I'm a man, at best pedestrian.
I say we both sequester
Till sometime next semester.

To Kill With Kindness

I tried to kill with kindness, though I failed, I fear to say:
The victims of my wrath are all still standing.
But I'm not giving up; in fact, I'm kinder every day,
Since any other method's too demanding.

The Tourist

The tourist with his luggage strolls
(At last, a leather bag that rolls!)
Along the walk that lines the port
Unswerving toward his luxe resort.

He enters through electric doors
(Thank God for all-inclusive tours!).
His travel quite conveniently
Shows only what he wants to see.

He stays locked in behind the gate
(This concierge is really great!)
And ventures out by private coach
Where locals likely won't approach.

He'll take in sites he saw in books
And offer nodding earnest looks,
And less than half-attention pay
To all the patient guide will say.

When his two weeks are nearly gone
(Can you believe this perfect lawn?)
He'll call the desk to hail a car
So he won't have to walk too far.

And as he boards the boat, then he
For just the second time will see
The lovely island where he stayed
Behind tall walls, ate, drank, and played.

He comes back home; now all is well
(Those first-class seats are mighty swell!)
Convinced that he, unlike most blokes,
Could live among the foreign folks.

He sees himself a wiser man,
Committed cosmopolitan.
One day he will the world explore
As long as there's a package tour.

Black and White and Unread All Over

There they sit on our shelves with the rest:
Dante, Milton, Marx, *Infinite Jest*
And *Ulysses.* We dread 'em,
For, though we ain't read 'em,
We're pressed to attest they're the best.

Birdbrain

I guess I could have overlooked the way she slurped her tea;
She wore outdated hair and clothes, the kind you never see.
Her taste in books and movies was benign, if quite absurd,
But then there was the matter of her idiotic bird.

She named him Harley Davidson, which says an awful lot;
She looked online for parrot toys, then bought and bought and
    bought.
Her voice was high and squeaky, though she sounded self-assured
Whenever she would talk about her idiotic bird.

Her language skills deserved at best a passing grade of Fair
For *irregardless, anyways,* and *there* instead of *their.*
I could care less was her reply when I'd correct a word,
And then I'd hear the chatter of her idiotic bird.

At music she was hopeless, as tone-deaf as one could be
(The albums on her shelf reflected this deficiency).
She'd try to sing but she'd be off at least a major third,
Which triggered yet more squawking from her idiotic bird.

One pet was not enough, of course; for some it never is—
She owned a dog, a cat or two, a rodent she named Liz.
All day and night that stupid hamster wheel just whirred and
    whirred,
Although it never could drown out her idiotic bird.

And so in time things ended just the way they had to end:
We swore to keep in touch and then we parted friend to friend.
I always said she'd have to choose between us—she demurred,
But when push came to shove she picked her idiotic bird.

Perspective

A woman may a goddess be,
   Yet she alone can't spot it;
A man whose failings only he
   Can't see thinks, "I've still got it!"

Unsafe at Any Speed

To double-cross the Don he tried,
But Sonny knew damn well he lied.
Clemenza took him for a drive
And he did not return alive.
You won't see him no more—that's Paulie.
Leave the gun, take the cannoli.

Then Carlo died in his new coat
With wire wrapped around his throat.
A car is *not* the place to be
With members of this family,
So use your head, not your cojones;
Never ride with Corleones!

Important

It's important you know I'm important;
  That's why I speak loud on my phone
In cafes, at a store, on the subway,
  Wherever—I'm never alone.

Is my colloquy audible? Perfect;
  For silence I don't give a damn,
And the fact there's no way to ignore me
  Just proves how important I am!

A Man of Inaction

God bless the king who one day said
I think I'll just go back to bed.
No war he launches in his sleep,
No soldiers die, no widows weep.
No lands are conquered, walls torn down,
No loot and pillage town to town.
No churches, barns, or castles fall,
No carnage in the realm at all.

The history books will surely say
He ruled his kingdom well that day;
Great wisdom did the sovereign show
In slumber oh so long ago.
Good fortune fell upon this chap,
And all because he took a nap.

The Editors Who Love My Work

The editors who love my work are few and far between;
Their ratio of *yes* to *no* is one-to-seventeen.
To laud these daring souls I now attempt to wax poetic:
They're mad enough to print the stuff steeped in my strange
    aesthetic.

The Name Game

With a name like Hieronymus
You'll be nonanonymous,
But not like Hippocrates,
Aurelius, or Socrates.
No tyrant Tyrolean
Could conquer Napoleon,
And clever Catullus
Was no Foster Dulles.

A String of Earls

I *hate* it when I'm called a "minor noble."
I say better to be either broke
Or rich—though rich is best—perhaps a global
Head of state (or both, a masterstroke).

Hereditary titles? They're a fluke;
How much power's in the nomenclature
Of Earl, of Regent, Baron, Count, or Duke?
I want more; that's merely human nature.

Do *not* mistake my reticence for shyness;
Deem me not a Viscount or Marquis.
One day I hope to hear "Your Royal Highness."
That's a title good enough for me!

Anarchist Club

On Tuesday next our club will meet
At Knightsbridge Road and Regent Street:
The Oxbridge League Society
For Propagating Anarchy.
There's fish and chips, of course a bar
(So middle-class, but there you are).
We have a revolution planned,
But hope it won't get out of hand.

Frustrations I have felt of late,
For things have not been going great.
I do my best, I do my part,
Yet meetings never seem to start
On time, and some weeks not at all.
Attendance has begun to fall,
While many fail to pay their dues;
What's more, I hear dissenting views
On plans of action, strategies,
And even core philosophies.

Around here I wear many hats,
But frankly it's like herding cats
To get these plotters on one page.
I do believe we've reached the stage
Committees must be formed, and then
More subcommittees. Maybe when
The chairs have all assumed their seats
We'll take this battle to the streets.

We mean to show our discontent
And overthrow the government;
We'll keep on meeting till that day
If *I* have anything to say.
You'd think our goals would be enough
To knit us tight, but man, it's tough
(Despite my many detailed lists)
To organize these anarchists!

Bread Alone

We do not live by bread alone, or so the Gospel tells,
   Though on this point I feel it's fairly fickle—
You *have* to try the marble rye our local baker sells,
   And you will not *believe* the pumpernickel!

The Cake Aisle of Applebee's

With apologies to W.B. Yeats

I will arise and go now, and go to Applebee's,
And a small order place there, of chicken waffles made;
A coffee will I have there, some pie and a slice of cheese,
And wait alone for the marmalade.

And I shall see Bernice there, Bernice who's moving slow,
Moving from the start of the morning to what the lunchtime brings;
There late shift's all a nuisance, the neon lights aglow,
Bernice untying her apron strings.

I will arise and go now, for always every day
I hear the senior discount saves ten percent or more;
While I stand at the counter, on carpet dirty grey,
I see suburban chain decor.

Customer Disservice

Your call is most important, friend;
  Please take a place in queue.
We can't say when your wait will end
  Or when we'll put you through.

Our cheery tone? It's by design;
  You'll be here quite a while.
Remain on hold to stay in line,
  Don't hang up and redial.

That little click; your sprits rise!
  But soon all hope is gone.
A rep will join you soon—pure lies
  To keep you hanging on.

Enjoy our music loud; we know
  This tune might bring you mirth.
The full song's more expensive, so
  We've looped eight seconds worth.

Would you have time when this is done
  To take a survey? We
Just want to be your Number One
  Phone service company!

The Market Is a Mistress Cold

The market is a mistress cold,
  Her love for me is naught:
Up go the stocks that I just sold,
  Down go the ones I bought.

Uneasy

You worry quite a lot, she says—I'm guilty on the whole.
   It's life, and trouble's always coming down.
Relax and take it easy! Ah, but that's not how I roll;
   Uneasy lies the head that wears the frown.

The Next Small Thing

I think that I shall never see
The Next Big Thing; it won't be me,
For fame and fortune don't beguile
And smaller better suits my style.

I am not Hamlet, nor was meant
To be—I understand this bent.
I need not play in any age
The cynosure at center stage.

Ambition I have kept in line;
Supporting roles will do just fine.
A Chorus or a walk-on part
Is really closer to my heart.

What's that you say? I've given up
And cannot hope to drain the cup
Of life, topped off for those who strive
To hit the heights while they're alive?

All glitter is not gold, my friends,
And this is where the story bends:
So many stars have short careers
But I'll get work for years and years.

About the Author

Steven Kent is the poetic alter ego of writer, musician, and Oxford comma enthusiast Kent Burnside (www.kentburnside.com). His work has been featured in *Light Poetry Journal, Lighten Up Online, New Verse News, Philosophy Now, Asses of Parnassus, Snakeskin, Hamlet Studies, Shakespeare in the Classroom, Fingerstyle Guitar 360,* and *The Nashville Musician,* where he also served as Assistant Editor. He has contributed more than 500 entries to the *Omnificent English Dictionary in Limerick Form (OEDILF).*